Is It Wrong to BAN BOOKS?

By Mary Austen

Published in 2018 by
KidHaven Publishing, an Imprint of Greenhaven Publishing, LLC
353 3rd Avenue
Suite 255
New York, NY 10010

Designer: Deanna Paternostro
Editor: Katie Kawa

Photo credits: Cover, p. 21 (inset, left) Africa Studio/Shutterstock.com; pp. 5, 11, 17, 21 (inset, right) wavebreakmedia/Shutterstock.com; p. 7 Neil Jacobs/Stringer/Getty Images News/Getty Images; p. 9 Jack R Perry Photography/Shutterstock.com; p. 13 (top) Yuganov Konstantin/Shutterstock.com; p. 13 (bottom) Monkey Business Images/Shutterstock.com; p. 15 Catalin Petolea/Shutterstock.com; p. 19 Ermolaev Alexander/Shutterstock.com; p. 21 (notepad) ESB Professional/Shutterstock.com; p. 21 (markers) Kucher Serhii/Shutterstock.com; p. 21 (photo frame) FARBAI/iStock/Thinkstock; p. 21 (inset, middle-left) Indigo Fish/Shutterstock.com; p. 21 (inset, middle-right) connel/Shutterstock.com.

Library of Congress Cataloging-in-Publication Data

Names: Austen, Mary, author.
Title: Is it wrong to ban books? / Mary Austen.
Description: New York : KidHaven Publishing, [2018] | Series: Points of view
  | Includes index.
Identifiers: LCCN 2017047480| ISBN 9781534524903 (6 pack) | ISBN
  9781534524279 (library bound book) | ISBN 9781534524897 (pbk. book)
Subjects: LCSH: Censorship–United States–Juvenile literature. | School
  libraries–Censorship–United States–Juvenile literature. | United
  States. Constitution. 1st Amendment–Juvenile literature. | Prohibited
  books–United States–Juvenile literature.
Classification: LCC KF4219 .A99 2018 | DDC 344.7305/31–dc23
LC record available at https://lccn.loc.gov/2017047480

Printed in the United States of America

CPSIA compliance information: Batch #CW18KL: For further information contact Greenhaven Publishing LLC, New York, New York at 1-844-317-7404.

Please visit our website, www.greenhavenpublishing.com. For a free color catalog of all our high-quality books, call toll free 1-844-317-7404 or fax 1-844-317-7405.

CONTENTS

Strong Feelings on
BOTH SIDES

Books are everywhere! You can buy books at bookstores, in grocery stores, and even on the Internet. Schools are filled with books to read, and libraries let you borrow books for free. Books tell stories and teach readers about many things.

Some people think books about certain things shouldn't be read by everyone—or read at all in some cases. Some people and even some governments around the world try to ban books they think are bad. Others believe it's wrong to keep people from reading books—no matter what they're about.

Know the Facts!

Banning books is a form of censorship, which is the practice of taking away or taking out parts of things, such as books, movies, or music, that people in power think are bad.

Many people think it's wrong to ban books, but some people have a different point of view. They think banning certain books **protects** people, especially children. It's good to understand why people feel the way they do—even if you don't agree with them.

Bans and
CHALLENGES

Throughout history, governments have banned books that they believed were **dangerous**. In the United States today, most efforts to ban books are led by individuals or small groups.

These efforts to ban books are known as challenges. The American Library Association (ALA), which is a group that keeps track of bans and challenges, has stated that most challenges don't work. Even though people try to get certain books taken out of classrooms or libraries, bans don't happen very often. In some cases, the arguments about challenges and bans go to court.

Know the Facts!

According to the ALA, parents challenge books more than any other person or group.

Some people want to do more than just ban books they think are harmful. They burn them in large fires to make a statement. Other people see burning books as a dangerous form of censorship.

First Amendment

FREEDOMS

People who speak out against challenging and banning books believe they're fighting for freedom. In the United States, certain freedoms are given to the people who live there through the Bill of Rights. This is the first 10 amendments, or changes, to the U.S. Constitution, which is the piece of writing that set up the U.S. government.

The First Amendment protects freedom of speech and freedom of the press, along with other basic freedoms. People who believe it's wrong to ban books believe doing so goes against the First Amendment.

Know the Facts!

In the 1982 case *Board of Education, Island Trees Union Free School District No. 26 v. Pico*, the U.S. Supreme Court ruled that a group couldn't ban books just because people didn't like the ideas in them.

Congress of the United States

begun and held at the City of New-York, on

Wednesday the fourth of March, one thousand seven hundred and eighty nine

THE Conventions of a number of the States, having at the time of their adopting the Constitution, expressed a desire, in order to prevent misconstruction or abuse of its powers, that further declaratory and restrictive clauses should be added: And as extending the ground of public confidence in the Government, will best ensure the beneficent ends of its institution.

RESOLVED by the Senate and House of Representatives of the United States of America, in Congress assembled, two thirds of both Houses concurring that the following Articles be proposed to the Legislatures of the several States, as amendments to the Constitution of the United States, all, or any of which Articles, when ratified by three fourths of the said Legislatures, to be valid to all intents and purposes, as part of the said Constitution, viz.

ARTICLES in addition to, and Amendment of the Constitution of the United States of America, proposed by Congress, and ratified by the Legislatures of the several States, pursuant to the fifth Article of the original Constitution.

Article the first..... After the first enumeration required by the first Article of the Constitution, there shall be one Representative for every thirty thousand, until the number shall amount to one hundred, after which, the proportion shall be so regulated by Congress, that there shall be not less than one hundred Representatives, nor less than one Representative for every forty thousand persons, until the number of Representatives shall amount to two hundred, after which the proportion shall be so regulated by Congress, that there shall not be less than two hundred Representatives, nor more than one Representative for every fifty thousand persons.

Article the second.... No law, varying the compensation for the services of the Senators and Representatives, shall take effect, until an election of Representatives shall have intervened.

Article the third.... Congress shall make no law respecting an establishment of religion, or prohibiting the free exercise thereof; or abridging the freedom of speech, or of the press, or the right of the people peaceably to assemble, and to petition the Government for a redress of grievances.

Article the fourth.... A well regulated militia, being necessary to the security of a free State, the right of the people to keep and bear arms, shall not be infringed.

Article the fifth.... No Soldier shall, in time of peace be quartered in any house, without the consent of the owner, nor in time of war, but in a manner to be prescribed by law.

Article the sixth.... The right of the people to be secure in their persons, houses, papers, and effects, against unreasonable searches and seizures, shall not be violated, and no warrants shall issue, but upon probable cause, supported by oath or affirmation, and particularly describing the place to be searched, and the persons or things to be seized.

Article the seventh.... No person shall be held to answer for a capital, or otherwise infamous crime, unless on a presentment or indictment of a Grand Jury, except in cases arising in the land or naval forces, or in the Militia, when in actual service in time of War or public danger; nor shall any person be subject for the same offence to be twice put in jeopardy of life or limb, nor shall be compelled in any criminal case to be a witness against himself, nor be deprived of life, liberty, or property

Article the eighth.... In all criminal prosecutions, the accused shall enjoy the right to a speedy and public ___ district shall have been previously ascertained by law, and to be informed of the nature ___ for obtaining witnesses in his favor, and to have the assistance of counsel for his d___

Article the ninth.... In suits at common law, where the value in controversy shall exceed twenty dollars, the ___ any Court of the United States, than according to the rules of the common law.

Article the tenth.... Excessive bail shall not be required, nor excessive fines imposed, nor cruel and unus___

Article the eleventh.... The enumeration in the Constitution, of certain rights, shall not be construed to deny or disparage others retained by the people.

Article the twelfth.... The powers not delegated to the United States by the Constitution, nor prohibited by it to the States, are reserved to the States respectively, or to the people.

ATTEST,

Frederick Augustus Muhlenberg Speaker of the House of Representatives.

John Adams, Vice President of the United States, and President of the Senate.

The ALA and other groups that are against banning books believe the freedom to read is protected in the Bill of Rights, shown here.

9

A School's
DECISION

Although some people believe groups such as governments and school boards shouldn't control what people read, others disagree. This is especially true for banning books in school libraries. Some people believe schools should be able to decide whether or not to ban books from their libraries.

People who feel this way argue that schools can choose what to teach in classes and what books to buy for libraries. They should then be able to choose what books to take out of their libraries if they find the content of those books **offensive**.

Know the Facts!

According to the ALA, half of all book challenges in 2016 happened in schools and school libraries.

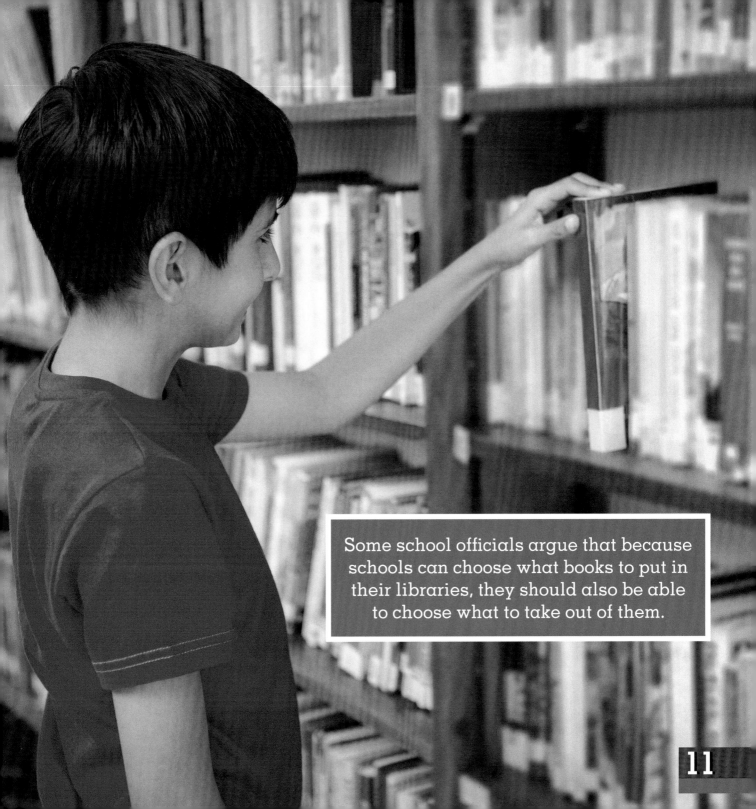

Some school officials argue that because schools can choose what books to put in their libraries, they should also be able to choose what to take out of them.

Books Are
TEACHERS

In the ALA's Library Bill of Rights, the group states that schools, librarians, and governments shouldn't be given the right to censor what young people read. Only parents or guardians should be allowed to decide what their children read.

Books that are challenged and banned often ask readers to think differently about the world around them. Many people argue that this is exactly why these books need to stay on shelves. Books should teach readers about different ways of thinking and living. Banning them makes it so people can only learn what those in power want them to learn.

Know the Facts!

In 2016, the ALA recorded 323 book challenges.

Instead of banning books, some people argue that books should be used to get people to think and talk to each other about **controversial** subjects.

Why Are Books
BANNED?

Books are banned and challenged for many reasons. The people who support these bans and challenges believe they're all good reasons. Drug use, offensive language, and **violence** are often reasons books are challenged or banned.

In some cases, books are banned because they deal with opinions on government and **religion** that people in power feel are harmful. Some people also believe books that deal with **racism** should be banned to keep readers from learning racist words and ideas.

Know the Facts!

From 2000 to 2009, the Harry Potter books by J.K. Rowling were the most commonly banned books in the United States because people didn't want kids reading books about witches and wizards.

Books that are challenged and banned are often thought to be filled with dangerous or upsetting language and ideas.

Different
VOICES

When books are banned, the people who ban them decide that some voices shouldn't be heard. In many cases, these voices are of writers who call attention to people, problems, and ideas that certain groups don't like.

Banning books that deal with subjects such as racism and disabilities keeps readers from finding stories that might help them understand the world and themselves better. If someone is dealing with these issues in their own life, reading a book about it might make them feel less alone. Banning books about it might make them feel bad for being different.

Know the Facts!

More than 50 percent of the books challenged between 2006 and 2016 had diverse content, which means they dealt with subjects such as race, religion, and living with a disability.

Books open people's minds. Banning them keeps
people from learning about different people and ideas.

Protecting
CHILDREN

Children's books might seem harmless, but they're often challenged or banned. They're sometimes banned because they deal with subjects people feel children shouldn't be learning about. These books aren't considered age appropriate, or right for the ages who are meant to read them.

Adults who challenge or ban children's books for this reason believe they're protecting children from things that might scare them or upset them. They might also believe they're keeping children from learning the wrong things or learning things before they're ready to know about them.

Know the Facts!

Where the Wild Things Are by Maurice Sendak is a popular children's book that has been banned by different groups because people feel it could be upsetting for children.

If a book might scare or upset some kids, certain people think no kids should read it. Do you think this is right?

People feel very strongly about banning books. Some people believe it's important to protect children and others from content they feel is dangerous. People on the other side of this **debate** feel it's important to protect the freedom to read and the freedom to **express** ideas without censorship.

These two points of view are very different, and the people on both sides believe they're doing the right thing. After learning the facts about and the reasons for and against banning books, what do you think? Is it wrong to ban books?

Know the Facts!

Banned Books Week has been celebrated every year since 1982. It was created to call attention to the censorship of books.

Is it wrong to ban books?

YES

- Banning books goes against the First Amendment.

- Only parents or guardians should decide what their children can and can't read.

- Books are important teachers, and banning books keeps readers from learning about different ideas and people.

- Banning books silences voices of writers who might make readers feel less alone for being different.

NO

- If schools can decide what books to put in their libraries and classrooms, they should be able to decide what books to take out of them.

- Banning books keeps young people from learning dangerous or offensive things.

- Banning books that deal with racism protects people from learning about racist ideas or language.

- Some children's books deal with subjects that are too scary or upsetting for the ages that are supposed to read them.

Creating a chart such as this one is a good way to make sense of the reasons people support or oppose a practice such as banning books.

GLOSSARY

controversial: Likely to create a disagreement.

dangerous: Not safe.

debate: An argument or discussion about an issue, generally between two sides.

express: To make thoughts and feelings known.

offensive: Causing someone to feel hurt, angry, or upset.

protect: To keep safe.

racism: The practice of treating others poorly because they are part of a different race, or group of people who look alike in certain ways.

religion: A set of beliefs about a god or gods.

violence: The use of force to harm someone.

For More
INFORMATION

WEBSITES

ALA Banned and Challenged Books

www.ala.org/advocacy/bbooks/frequentlychallengedbooks/statistics
This part of the ALA website allows visitors to see the most commonly challenged books over the last few years, as well as the reasons why those books were challenged and where those challenges took place.

Banned Books Week

www.bannedbooksweek.org/
The official website for Banned Books Week features facts about censorship, commonly banned and challenged books, and events celebrating the right to read.

BOOKS

Cahill, Bryon. *Freedom of Speech and Expression*. South Egremont, MA: Lerner Publishing Group, 2014.

Dell, Pamela. *You Can't Read This!: Why Books Get Banned*. Mankato, MN: Compass Point Books, 2010.

Mason, Jenny. *Freedom of Speech*. New York, NY: Gareth Stevens Publishing, 2017.

INDEX

I dedicate this book to my friend
and "sister" - Jillian Namatjirra.

Margo

MARGO STANISLAWSKA-BIRNBERG

Journeylines

Photographs:
JANUSZ B. KRECZMANSKI and MARGO STANISLAWSKA-BIRNBERG

J.B. BOOKS AUSTRALIA

Journeylines

This hard cover first edition is an exclusive production published in the year 2000
by J.B. Books Pty Ltd
P.O. Box 118
Marleston 5033
South Australia
Phone/Fax (08) 8297 1669

National Library of Australia
Cataloguing in Publication data:

Birnberg, Margo
Journeylines
ISBN 1 876622 11 3

1. Aborigines, Australia
2. Poetry
3. Aboriginal Artists

Book design concept: Janusz Kreczmanski
Graphic design: Robert Moller
Editing: Margo Birnberg
Printing and Production through Phoenix Offset
Printed in Hong Kong

"The author wishes to thank the owners of copyright for their kind permission to reproduce
the photographs in this book"

Front Cover:

Left to Right - Top: Emily Kame Kngwarreye, Cassidy Tjapaltjarri, Archie Roach.
- *Centre:* Ruby Hunter, Pansy Napangati, Ada Bird Petyarre.
- *Below:* Edward Blitner, Lily Hargraves Nungarrayi, Clifford Possum Tjapaltjarri.

CONTENTS

Back cover: M.F. Stanislawska-Birnberg (Biographical note)

Road to Kalkarinji

From the author

I hope my poetry will give readers a better understanding and appreciation of the Australian Aborigines. I have great regard for the people of the desert region and I love the Australian deserts. When one looks at the map of Australia it becomes rather obvious how easy it is to indulge in that passion. Nearly three quarters of this continent is covered by desert. What is there to love? The beauty of the desert is more elusive. I love the solitude, the danger of the remote region, the crystal clear air, the feeling of being the only human around for thousands of square kilometres. Putting up with this harsh environment brought me closer to the desert dwellers, the Australian Aborigines. I have been travelling in this region for the past twenty-five years. All these years gave me, I hope, a better understanding of the Aborigines. My greatest wish became a reality when an elder of a Warlpiri tribe acknowledged me as a tribal member.
Now I belong to the white and to the black race. I am trying to understand both.

Writing a book is an all-involving process. Whatever we do, there are other people to help, give advice or inspire us. I was lucky to find many such kind friends and acquaintances. Foremost I would like to thank all my Aboriginal friends, especially Clifford Possum Tjapaltjarri, Emily Kame Kngwarreye, Lily Sandover, the three Petyarre sisters from Utopia : Ada Bird, Gloria and Nancy, Mick Namerari from Kintore, the potters from Hermannsburg and their adviser Naomi Sharp, Eunice Napangardie, Pansy Napangati, Mary Dixon Nungarrayi, Lily Hargraves Nungarrayi from Lajamanu, Ronny Jagamarra's and Louisa Napaltjarri's family from Mangurrulpa, and Edi Blitner from the Mara-Alawa near Roper River. In Alice Springs I found great understanding and helpful advice from Janice Stanton and Daphne Williams from Papunya Tula Gallery, Iris Harvey, a friend for many years (an Alice Springs identity from Arunta Bookshop), and Michael Hollows from Aboriginal Art Gallery. My thanks go to Glenis Wilkins and family and Harold and Colleen Raunacher for their hospitality when I was in dire need of a bed after many days roughing it. I will never forget the moment when I read my poem "Coorong Girl" to Archie Roach and he cried in remembrance of his own childhood. His words: *"You understand it, Margo"*, gave me a will and strength to go on with my writing. I wish to thank Ruby Hunter for teaching me her precious words of the Ngarrindjeri, Professor Jerzy (George) Zubrzycki who, very willingly in spite of his busy schedule, took upon himself the task of writing the foreword. Geoffrey Bardon read my poems and kindly praised my effort in trying to understand the Aboriginal people. A special thank you to my friend, Janusz B. Kreczmanski, for always believing in me and for the encouragement he gave me over the years. To John Brakel, my publisher for taking a chance.

It helps to have an understanding family and I was blessed with one, so thank you to my husband Jacques for putting up with my long absences when I travelled in the bush and to my three sons: Olaf, Conrad and Alexander.

Margo Stanislawska-Birnberg

Foreward

As we approach the Millennium and Centenary of Federation Australians must face some stark nation-defining choices. Either we take a real shot at being a harmonious, inclusive and fair society or we become a totally divided one. The theme of the Reconciliation Convention - Renewal of the Nation - must be placed high on the agenda of those of us who wish to promote a model of a just society.

Margo Stanislawska-Birnberg's poetry is an excellent example of the place the Reconciliation with Aboriginal Australians should have in articulating and strengthening the Australian multicultural achievement. The quality of her poetry is one that William Carlos Williams once called "the essential naivete of a poet".

Against the bleak realities of Aboriginal deprivation that she observes, the poet places what is still possible: how the Ancestors' Dreaming in the corroborees of the Central Desert and in the veins of the artist Mick Namerrari can be reconciled with the need to "decipher power and phone bills" and other ways of the white men.

The naivete of the poet serves Margo Stanislawska-Birnberg well. It enables her to understand the invocations of Dreaming in the harshness of the desert: in the timeless features of the rivers of sand with their "dripping dryness", in the stony maiden of the ancestral Pintubi land with its White Dingo Dog Spirit - the "totem rock gleaming white" - and even in the abandoned railway settlement on the Indian-Pacific line - now in the throes of death - its fate "stamped by restructuring economy". Margo Sanislawska-Birnberg's poetry is also a moving testimony of a Polish migrant who on the day of her naturalisation "became a citizen before the original Australian" (Paradoxes - 1963).

> I had full rights
> Before to them they were given
> I did not realise then
> There were questions to be asked
> That I would discover history
> Shaming the "pillars" of the society.

The poet's journey of discovery is documented in this volume in which "the essential naivete" of her craft helps her to highlight the humanity that should link us all in the pluralist Australia. If renewal of the Nation is to be more than a slogan then clearly all Australians must strive to acquire the insights that alone can help us to understand what Dreaming is all about. Margo Stanislawska-Birnberg's poetry is not an insignificant contribution to our national endeavour. This is what multiculturalism must stand for - the pursuit of justice, fairness, civility and decency for all Australians.

Professor Jerzy (George) Zubrzycki
Member, National Multicultural Advisory Council

Billy Stockman Tjapaltjarri

1

Tjulkurra, in Anmatyerre language means, one with grey hair.

The Tjulkurra-
Billy Stockman Tjapaltjarri

Trachoma invading his eyes
Hands slowing down and stiffening
Legs too tired to carry his years
But the old Tjulkurra still has his smile.
Good morning, how are you?
Greets me every day
And when I recall the Anmatyerre word he taught me
He nods with approval his snow-white head.
Yowi, yes, you got that one,
Palya lingka, it's a good one, he says
Precious words from his childhood
Punctuate his proper sounding English accented speech.
But Billy's long life is still overshadowed
In remembrance of his younger days
When only just a baby
He survived a massacre in a coolamon hidden.
Dark days of 1928
When familiar sandhills reverberated to guns
Bad deeds in Coniston cannot be forgotten
Tribal members perished among the dunes.
Punitive posse with vengeful hearts
Galloped from distant place.
Unsuspecting and untroubled
Small family groups camped by a riverbed.
Children's laughter rang in clear desert air,
The smoke of fires rose high to the moon
Clapping of sticks and chanting of men
Mingled with sounds and smells of the bush.
Then shrieks and confusion.
Cries of lost children.
Hooves flailing.
Report of guns.
Pounding feet.
Dying and dead
Heaped on one bank.
Stench of burning flesh.
One small baby whimpering quietly
In bushes, hastily concealed by mother's loving care.

Margo and Billy

Palmer River, Northern Territory

Rivers of Sand

Avenues of river gums stretching into the distance,
By their presence they promise precious water down below.
Brumby, maddened with thirst
Fruitlessly digs for it with desperate hooves.

Loose sand grains not bound with liquid gold,
Like in an hour-glass, relentlessly, keep falling down
Then shifted by wind from their river-home
Form intricate patterns of delicate beauty.

Playthings for the whirlwind
Who catches them unaware
And scatters the wavy forms
Among the dunes.

Rivers of sand, your timeless features
Not disturbed by flowing waves
Like figments of one's imagination
Your dreams are seldom fulfilled.

Unsteady borders of dripping dryness,
Rustling of leaves instead of moving rains,
The eye seeks but never finds
A droplet to quench a thirst.

Napperby Lakes" by Clifford Possum Tjapaltjarri

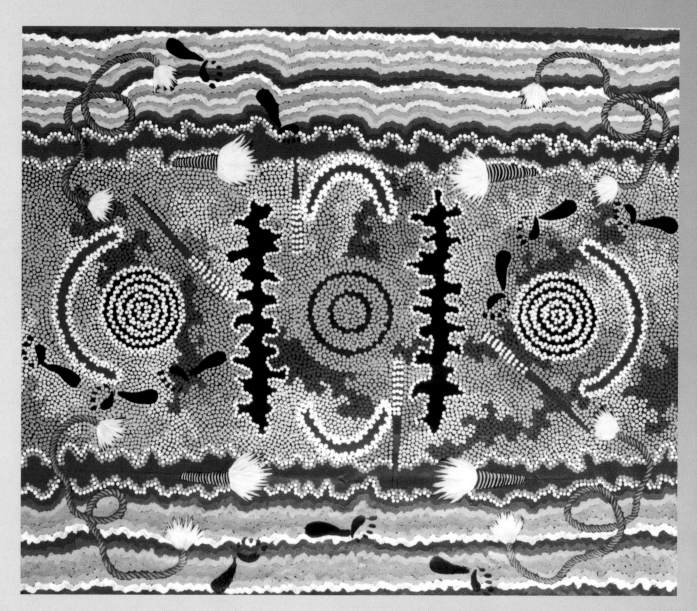

"Men's Corroboree Dreaming" by *Clifford Possum Tjapaltjarri*

I spent many evenings in the Central and Western deserts watching corroborees. It was a spectacle which became imprinted on my mind. The smell of the fire, the warm sand, the rising dust from beneath the stamping feet of the dancers, the rhythmic click-clack of the music-sticks and the hollow sounds coming from the motion of the women pounding their thighs.

All that dancing and singing, which was happening in front of my eyes, was exciting and memorable but the meaning of it incomprehensible to me. The women tried very patiently to explain the stories re-enacted, to no avail. And then the moment came when I at last understood a small part of it.

I will try to understand more.

Dance,
A Sudden Understanding

flicker of flames on intent faces
sparks burning into watchful eyes
shuffle, rhythmic shuffle of feet
line of moving bodies

the dust rises and envelops the dancers feet

thighs pulsating, beating of hands
in rhythms with the stamping,
voices flow over the moving sand
and invade the still air of the night

Your heart, you thought, was dead to it all

it now stirs to the sounds
all awake and receptive
it beats faster,
an echo to the evocations of the Dreaming

with the sudden understanding it becomes a pain so great

that you must release it and shout
or you feel, the life force will ebb away.
You jump up and join the line,
imitate the movements,
your body and mind willing
but without the deeper knowledge
you flounder, but you try

Stuart Highway near Tennant Creek

7

Written after passing Port Augusta in South Australia and 'hitting' the Stuart Highway.

Stuart Highway

A straight ribbon of tar cutting in half the horizon
Thunder of rubber taking me forward
Five meters of civilisation and city dweller's safety
Immense desert on both sides hemming me in.

Port Augusta with the blue finger of Spencer Gulf behind me
My eyes turned towards the centre of Australia
It looks so easy to clock the distance
With a tank full of petrol
And a wallet bulging with credit cards.

But the unknown to me, so, savage and dangerous
Lurks just behind the first line of bushes
Dry hot wind and the round ball of the sun
Can break my city courage.

Black wings of the ever ready crows
Hover above the red sandhills,
white salt lakes
and men made security.

Sturt's Desert Pea

Salt Lake in South Australia

Written in Pimba, a little dot of a settlement in South Australia. John McDouall Stuart, an Australian explorer, believed that there was a vast inland sea which he called Kindur. He searched in vain. Stuart Highway carries his name and Pimba is an oasis on that road.

Salt Lakes

I saw past Pimba a watery horizon,
Stuart's dreaming of Kindur, an inland sea,
Full of welcoming water.
Framed by distant hills like pinch-pleated curtains.

With all the abundance of life giving liquid
No birds sat on its surface,
No fish showed gleaming scales,
No flowers edged its shores,
Only long fingers of the sun
Played on the golden mirror.
The rays, long drinking straws,
Left a white crust behind,
Like a diet conscious woman
Who rejects whipped cream.

Kingoonya, South Australia

Kingoonya is a small railway settlement on the Indian-Pacific line in South Australia.

Kingoonya

Straining nails against corrugated iron
Torn clothing flapping on a bend clothes-line
Shards of broken glass gleaming between rusted car parts.

Child's go-cart abandoned
Memory of a garden edged with stones in flaking paint
Gaping panel- less windows.

A lone caretaker walks the diminishing lanes and streets
Waiting now only for tourists
Who may never come.

No dogs annoyingly barking
Only kangaroo shooters invading the nights
Houses moving out on big tracks to outlaying sheep stations.

Kingoonya, an unfulfilled dream
Lives only in memories of people scattered
Glimpses of the past in fading photos glued in family albums.

The Indian-Pacific line still gleams
For the occasional train that rushes by
The famous 'Straight' in the throes of death
Fate stamped by restructuring economy.

*Coober Pedy - the
opal capital,
South Australia*

*Coober Pedy -
opal mines*

*Coober Pedy -
underground
shops*

Coober Pedy is an opal town in South Australia, a place where nature was made to yield its treasures.

Coober Pedy

Secrets the Earth was hiding
The colour dreams of old time heroes
Baimi's rainbow in friendship given
Then in anger smashed and buried.
The token of feelings
Lays now scattered for all to gloat over.
Desert undisturbed which slumbered for eons,
Pitjantjatjara's ancestral lands
Awaked by machinery
Tearing into the delicate flesh
Pure white and glistening in the noon-sun.
Vanity, vanity pushes the miner deeper into the ground.
Tired eyes, torn by gelignite flesh
Beautiful greens, reds, golds
Adorning fingers and necks.

Moon Plain

15

A desolate place between Coober Pedy and Oodnadatta, South Australia, was the exercise ground for future astronauts.

Moon Plain

Ancient heroes, why did you obliterate your creation
Like a sand painting you did not approve of ?
With impatient hand you flattened the earth,
Ground the mountains into brown dust.

Was it to hide some wondrous beauty
With the parched ugliness above?
Have you concealed the transformed rainbow
The vapour of the ancient creative breath ?

Mirages soften the harsh horizon,
A promise of water close at hand,
Nature conspires to lure you away
Further and further into the powdery dust.

Shadows of white explorers pass by you
With thoughts of glory and drink.
The Aborigine followed ancestors' tracks
With sure feet in all this bleakness.

The distant hills still dancing
Twirling dervishes in the waving air,
"Moon Plain" unfolds, like ploughed earth, waiting for seeds
Dispensed by its harsh master, then dissolves into the sky.

Summer whirlwinds imitate campfire smoke
Of the long vanished tribesmen.
The twisting cloud of flying dust pauses for a millisecond
Then passes by whispering some timeless secret.

Ancient heroes, which sacred dance might please you
And will bring lifes, back to this abandoned plain?

Alice Springs, in the background Heavitree Gap.

"White Dingo Dog Spirit Place", a story recounted to me by Raymond, a relative of Clifford Possum Tjapaltjarri. These secret Dreaming sites are still venerated by Aboriginal people in Central Australia.

The Gap

You walk across the Heavitree Gap
You trample the earth
The Aborigine winces
Caterpillar Dreaming again is disturbed.

"White Dingo Spirit" dreams on Gillen Mountain
His totem rock gleaming white
Larapinta Valley his stomping ground
Next to McDonald's his paw mark.

Don't touch the rock.
Let sleeping dogs lay.
The custodian warns the white man.
Don't come too close, somebody might die.

You laugh your smart arse laughter,
Don't pay attention. It's only blacks' talk.
That night a siren awakes you
And your friend now lies dead.

Gillen Mountain, Alice Springs

Todd River Gums, Alice Springs

Beautiful Todd River "flows", occasionally, through Alice Springs, Northern Territory.
Anangu are a tribal people from Central Australia.

Todd River Gums

Touched by countless sun filled days
Submerged when a seedling by flash floods
Growing strong with far outreaching branches
Giving shade to sacred dances.

Swaying to ancient rhythms
Whispering remembered tunes
Dropping bark to stretch bulging trunk
Reaching high into the cloudless sky.

Old tribesman dreams of his Tjukurrpa
His gnarled hand matching your skin
Your sap slowing in your veins
Every thunderstorm proclaiming your doom.

Days and years pass quickly as seasons
Anangu still try out your shade
But your arms once so powerful
Drop now lifelessly by your side.

Eunice Napangardi painting her Dreaming

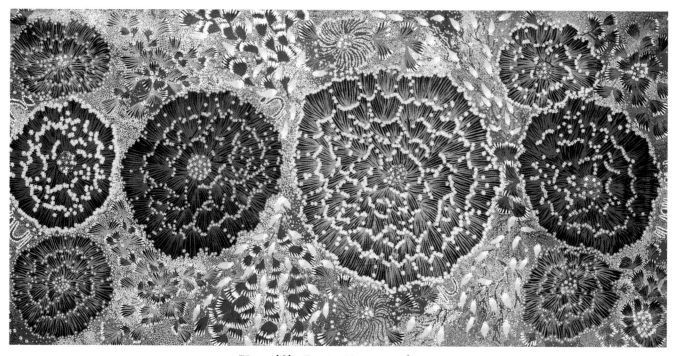

"Yuparli" by Eunice Napangardi

Based on a story sung to me by Eunice Napangardi. Yuparli is a Warlpiri name for bush bananas,
native fruit growing in Central Australia. Eunice very often paints the Dreaming story associated with
yuparli ceremonies.

Yuparli

Yuparli, your small flowers proclaiming your birth .
An old, lovelorn man
Trying to seduce his niece.

Napangardie and Napanangka women
In their coolamons winnowing seeds,
To the seducer's song are closing their ears.

Yuparli, you are growing stronger.
But the old man's love is unfulfilled
With white string he bounds his sorry head.

Women's derisive laughter
Echoes around the windbreaks.
Yuparli, your season's coming to fruition
These two women not ravished by the man.

His forlorn figure, alone,
At the abandoned desert camp.

Eunice Napangardi

Bush Banana - Yuparli

22

Mary Dixon Nungarrayi painting Bush Plum Dreaming

23

I saw a horse, painted with a sure hand, on a tin shed at Morris' Soak. Later, in an Alice Springs mall,
I noticed three old Aboriginal men perusing post cards on a stand.

The Painted Horse

Among the discarded coolabah cartons
Brown horse is prancing
On the white corrugated iron wall
His mane in the wind is dancing.

Hooves pounding the invisible grass
Broken bottles, shinning like desert suns
The stallion snorts with rage
Feeble hands can't hold the reins.

Old feet now dragging
Muscles stiff and withered
Dreams of long gone stockmen's days
Reverberate in the head.

Three old men stopped in an Alice Spring's Mall
In front of a postcard stand
A photo of Old Andado Station
Bringing to them mixed memories and pain.

They fondle the postcard closely
Pointing to broken down fence
Youthful smiles stretch the wrinkles
Parched skin recalls stockmen's days.

Old Andado Station lives for them forever
Recalled time and time again
The days are gone of braking horses
Only the painted one lets them dream again.

Coolabah Tree

Soaks

Swaying to white men's water,
Tongue twisted,
Language forgotten.

The seed sown strong
In generations before,
In you have weakened.

Knees bend.
Eyes vacant.

Desert breath
Left your lungs.

Reality obliterated.

Coolabah is not a tree any more.
Uncorked, it dripped into your mind.

Ancestors call unanswered
Is dying, alone among the dunes.

Abbot's Soak, Morris' Soak, Charles' Creek,
Once spirit meeting places,
Now roar to your mixed up tunes.

Todd River Gum, Alice Springs

*Australian bush regenerates itself, miraculously, after a searing fire. The hold on life and the push
to survive is always a marvel to watch. River gums are especially good at it .*

Tenacious

Crazed fire chews up living flesh
Sap explodes in orange tongues
Voracious teeth gnaw into roots
Trunk splits open in mortal wounds
Smouldering blackness
Gapes with unseeing eyes
Hot air presses into tearing skin
Surrealist sculpture in living, dying frame.

One filament of persistent survival
Bursts into green flame.

Desert Rose

Cemetery in Hermannsburg, Northern Territory

Aluminium Cans

New flowers have grown
On the red dune sand
Proclaiming anguish and pain.

Hunters prostrate body
Across the kangaroo track
An over-turned car spewing petrol
Cry of a hurt child
Broken moans from under the chassis.

Dust settles down again
Tyre marks obliterated by the wind
Another small, red mound
At the local cemetery.

New flowers now grow
Among the aluminium cans
A family torn apart by a drinking binge.

Simpson Desert from the air

Pansy Napangati

Nature's abundance on canvas is teeming
Intricate patterns call out their name
Strange fruits, trees, flowers emerging
Under the guidance of Pansy's hand.

The painter's eyes follow the story
Soft colours cover sharp thorns
Dry rivers meander over ancestral land
Pansy's memories so vivid and eloquent.

Group of Tingari Dreamtime women
Sitting together bound by creation
Grandfather's country fondly remembered
In Pansy's painting and imagination.

Pansy Napangati and her Dreaming

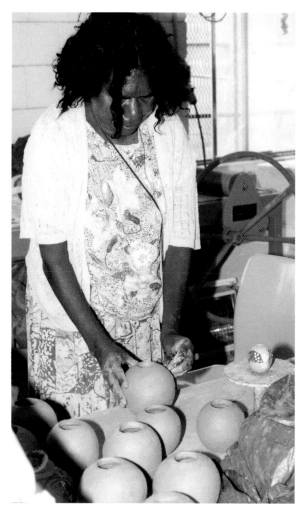

Hermannsburg potters, Hermannsburg

Hermannsburg Potters

Red earth in caring embrace.
Small spatula scraping surface.
Shape is emerging in slow motion.
Whirring of motors
does not disturb the pace.
Circle of women
their voices a sing song
build with patience small pots from clay.

Then colours of blue sky,
Clouds, little lizards, yellow frogs,
black dots on smooth skin,
cackling of cockatoos, smell of wattles
all emerge from under skilful hands.

Naomi, Hermannsburg potters' adviser and Margo

The Ochre Pits (118km West of Alice Springs). The ochre from these pits was used by Aborigines for traditional body painting, decoration and trading.

The initiation ceremony for young boys, a very important part of growing up for Aboriginal youths, is men's business only.

Red Ochre Men

A furtive glance from behind,
Hushed voices, eyes roving around.
It's men's business only
For women not to know.
Initiation time for young boys.

Red Ochre Men are coming
Timeless secrets will be re-enacted
And boys made into men.
Cut with a stone into their ignorant bodies
Stories of long time Tjukurrpa.

The Sacred Red Ochre
Strength and manhood personified
Smeared on with an eagle feather.
To the neophytes revealed knowledge
Of generations coming from the Dreamtime.

An Eagle Ancestor flying over
The deep ravine of Serpentine Gorge
Guarding his secret, tribal territories.
His shadow falls over the ochre pits
Dripping with red, white and yellow.

Coolamon and painted stones

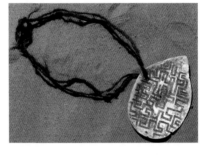

Churinga-ceremonial pearl shell pendant

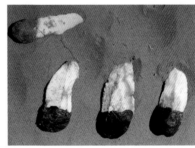

Stone knives

Corroboree Rock, Mac Donnell Ranges - Central Australia

I watched my little son Olaf tackling a rocky outcrop, to him a great mountain, to us, a mysterious formation. When he scrambled out on the other side I realised it was not just a climb but a repetition of an important initiation ceremony for boys.

Corroboree Rock

From the soft, shallow valley
Sprinkled with shade trees, strewn with reddish sand
Small figure scrambles towards the jagged outline of the Corroboree Rock.
Unsure legs wobble on upturned boulders
But the convex of the rock sends warm beaconing welcome.

Child's wriggling body climbs through a cleft,
Which opens like a womb before him.
He suddenly disappears from view
And meets the anxious eyes of the mother on the other side.

A deep, long valley stretches now in front of him.
On the horizon he sees a chain of mountains.
Winds bend weak trees that grow among them.
The strong ones lift up their limbs.

The little boy hears the wail of his mother
But curiosity guides faltering steps.
A squeeze along the narrow passage,
The vulnerable body slips across
The shiny lips of the split.
One step taken forward
And new worlds are unfolding.
Playful childhood must be now left behind.

Other bodies had worn smooth that path
In times of ancient wisdom
And drank knowledge with newly opened minds.

Hugh River, Central Australia

After a fifth punctured tyre, leaking petrol tank and a broken shock absorber, I surrendered.
I sat on the banks of a dry river and wept unashamedly .

Corrugations

Sand ripples unfolding
Buffeted by constant wind
Corrugated iron invented
By nature's chaotic hand.

Deadly for cars, trucks and tractors
Unrelenting and unforgiving
Shatters the hardest metals
Untwists the tightest bolts.

Wipers, windscreens and pipes
Car parts litter the bush tracks
The derelict wrecks a testimony
To the power of water and wind.

The Dry

Red desert sand shifts with moving wind
Twisting and turning to tin whistle tunes
Sharp barbs of spinifex find soft spots on your skin
Eyes smart from exposure to contrasting light
Distant hills dissolve their shape in midday heat
Trees float mid-air in belly-dancers moves.

Parched earth cracks under the strain
Grasses wither, then loose their heads
Rocks groan at night then fall apart
In maddened madrigals debils-debils
Fly across dissolved horizon
The "dry" squeezes last drops
Deposited by generous previous season.

Chambers Pillar - Itirkawara

43

Chambers Pillar, a fantastically shaped hill in Central Australia, was sighted in 1860 by the explorer John McDouall Stuart. Aboriginal Dreamtime stories say that it is the body of a Gecko Ancestor, Itirkawara, turned into a pillar of sandstone for his misdeeds.

Chambers Pillar

A beacon stands out in the desert
Rocky lighthouse without a keeper
The restless sun imitates the bulb
Moonshine reflects off its planed surface.

A menhir left by ancient creators
Eagerly sought by early explorers
For countless eons passed by tribesmen
Pointing the way for weary travellers.

Scratched names at base
A testament to courage or foolhardiness.
In disregard for past owners
Given a foreign sounding name.

Not far distant flowing sandhills
Guarding approach from Maryvale Station
Simpson Desert's hot breath fanning
Sparse vegetation and mulga's stunted branches.

Tourists now sit sometime on warm, red sand
And take photos to show off back at home
Silence broken by occasional bellowing of scrub bulls
Moon rise and sun set the constant changing of guards.

Chambers Pillar, Simpson Desert, Northern Territory

44

Clouds over Red Hill, Tanami Desert

Desert sunset

When we travelled in the Outback, I spun all kinds of stories to my three sons to keep them amused.

Clouds - A Sky Show

Timid one becomes a hero
Little mouse sprouts eagle's wings
Knights re-enact titanic battles
Gnashing their teeth with mighty strain.

Vanilla ice cream drips to the West side
Strawberry flavour comes from the East
The most bizarre and the commonest
For every wish and every dream.

The fiercest battles end in soft feathers
Maiden plaits her orange hair
Horse prances centre stage
Dragon breezes fire through air.

Watery crown in shape of a droplet
Strange figures, numbers, a fortunes wheel
All twist and turn, then change directions
Shapes become real then disappear.

Mighty wind smoothes the surface
All become one in shades of grey
Then a clap of thunder announces a spectacle
"*Son et Lumiere*", the rains are here.

Tanami Track

After being licked close to madness by flies during the day, and nearly being sucked dry of blood at night by mosquitos, I ruminated on the subject of planning.

****"!!* & *#*"***

Beautiful sunset
Vivid colours
Orange fights with evening shade
You open your mouth to exclaim in wonder
And all that comes out is a swear word.

Morning dews
Still cling to flowers
Fresh wind cools your face
In great amazement at nature's bounty
You want to say your thanks
You open your mouth to exclaim in wonder
And all that comes out is a swear word.

Milky Way
Blazes with star lights
Southern Cross points the way
Myriad of suns blink in darkness
With all that beauty you are amazed
You open your mouth to exclaim in wonder
And all that comes out is a swear word.

You are thankful and you are grateful
For all the riches nature gave
But why, you wonder, for blasted blazes
The fly and the mosquito came to be on Earth!

Mulga ants nest

Margo and the "sleeping woman"

A mountain on the road to Kintore and not far from Mt.Liebig looks like a sleeping woman. If one comes closer to investigate, she disappears from view.

An Illusion

A woman dreams in the mountains
A rock for a pillow
Stones in her hair
The wind ruffles leaves on her bosom
The rain washes her feet.

Rushing sands carved her features
The sun baked her face
An endless sleep in solitude
The near by ranges her next of kin.

Who will awaken the stony maiden?
Move her heart?
Smooth her hair?
A lonely tribesman trudges alongside
Looking for water not a dream.

Road to Kintore

Taking Mick Namerari to his place in Kintore allowed me to get to know this great and dignified man.
"Kapi pulka" in Pintubi language means - "plenty of water".

Car Journey to Kintore

The drone of the car is taking us further
Towards old Mick's Pintubi lands
Hot summer oppresses our bodies with heat
Water canister passes from hands to lips.

Mick waves his hand in certain direction
No words are spoken, thoughts understood.
We stop near large, granite boulders
To look for a soak preserved like a loot.

The earth is powdery dry
No breath of wind stirs the air
No birds darken the sky
Only the sandy road lies ahead.

Finger pointed with sureness and pride
Towards the Warrapulpa Range
Quiet words, so welcomed, encourage us
Kapi, kapi pulka there!

Country style music blares from the radio
Young generation sways at the back
Old Mick's young son asleep on father's knee
The Old Man fondly touches his cheek.

The desert oaks dance to summer tunes
Softly moaning in the hot desert winds
Their leaves like women's dancing skirts
It's Mick Namerari's ancestral Pintubi land.

Mick Namerari

Mingajurra means desert mouse in Pintubi language.

Mick Namerari - A Pintubi

On old Mick's weather beaten face
Pintubi ancestry in his features is engraved
With great dignity he observes the changing world.

Eyes that had seen pristine deserts
Tribal ways, free air and sky
Now try to decipher power and phone bills.

At Marpni, Mick's spirit place
Among the sandhills and spinifex
Passed happy childhood days.

Mission rations at Haast Bluff and Hermannsburg
Then initiation at Areyonga
Started his working stockman's years.

But old ways were not forgotten
Ancestors' Dreaming in his veins
Old Mick puts on canvass stories, legends and his dreams.

Mingajurra leaps across a square of linen
Kangaroo and Dingo Tjukurrpa illuminate a gallery wall
Mick Namerari is an artist and a tribal Pintubi still.

Louisa and Ronnie with the painting of "Medicine Vine"

Mangurrulpa

Mangurrulpa - minute grain in sandy ocean
Unknown to tourists travelling the Tanami Track.
Beloved country of Ronnie Jagamarra's and Louisa Napaltjarri's.
Covered with stunted mulga trees,
Sprinkled with clumps of spinifex.
Hot, dry and dusty.
Few gnarled trees with sparse shade,
Claypan with seasonal, infrequent water.
Dear to the heart of tribesmen,
Never willingly left or forgotten.
"Mongrel Downs" white fellas called it.
Like half-breed treated.
All they could feel was harshness of seasons,
Dying sheep, cunning dingo's pads,
Broken blades of windmills,
But not the reddish, soft sand under the feet,
Bush turkey's silent flight,
Spinifex pigeon's soft whirring of wings,
Grevillea dripping with honey,
Medicine Vine twisting body hugging a trunk,
Hopping mouse's mad dash
To safe little heaven in shade,
Majestic bounce of red kangaroo
And blue flyer's faithful tracks,
Rolling clouds bringing precious moisture,
Sudden rains pounding parched earth,
Bursting flowers later fecundate with seeds,
Sleepy frogs coming out from dried-out dreams,
Puddles teeming with wriggling bodies,
Wedge-tailed eagle's sweeping menace.
All over it watching, silent guardian of tribal secrets,
Rainbow Serpent coiled in a cave.

Medicine Vine

Women from Mt Allan digging for honey ants

Honey ants

Kvatch and ngapa are two different Aboriginal words both meaning water, Warrumpi means honey ant.

Honey Ants

Molly Napangardi sways in a dance
Two Napurrulas beat rhythm with sticks
Annie Nungarrayi sweeps out with her hands
The hidden chambers of the honey ants.

Crowbar's thuds hit the hard earth
Dust envelops the crouching women
The red, compacted sand
Does not want to release the sweetness from within.

Give me kvatch, ngapa, gasps Annie,
That cheeky ant went plenty way down.
No recent rains enticed the insect workers
To bring the live larders close to the surface.

A little twig pushed into chambers
Tweaks out the helpless yellow bellies
Coolamon brimming with delicate honey
Warrumpi Tjukurrpa re-enacted all over again.

Clifford Possum Tjapaltjarri

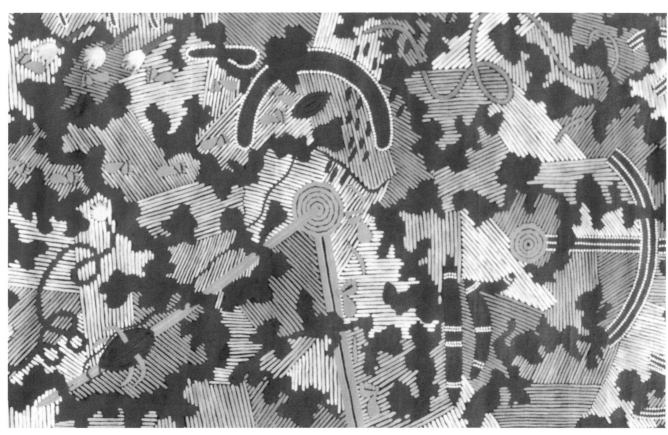

"Ngalu Tjukurpa" by Clifford Possum Tjapaltjarri

59

Big jumble of rocks strewn on grassy plain, not far from Yuelamu Honey Ant Dreaming site, conceals a moving story of "wrong skin" lovers.

Red Hill - Ngalu Tjukurrpa

Ngalu Tjukurrpa is one of Cassidy Tjapaltjarri's Dreamings. In his words, it is a big story, a proper one and very important. Clifford Possum Tjapaltjarri beautifully depicts this moving tale in his paintings. Cassidy and Clifford are tribal brothers.

Nangala rejected cursed her treacherous lover
With vengeance greater than a woman scorned.
His penis severed lies in a trench,
By his side, into rock transformed beloved.

With thighs quivering in untrammelled passion,
Lips open and ready to moan
No sound can escape and release the love
Loved one and loving turned into stone.

Against the wishes of tribal elders
Forbidden love began to bloom
Furtive looks and signs exchanged
A man and a woman sealed their doom.

Punishment dwelt swiftly
Laws must not be broken
Love not sanctioned will be banned
Ancient creators demand obedience
Ngalu Tjukurrpa - Red Hill Dream.

Young man, alone, sits on a rock ledge
On his thigh, from his hair, he twists a string.
A song repeated, on and on, proclaims his love to the wind
How long will I have to wait for my beloved?
How much warmth can I get from a stone?

Young woman, eager for a night of passion
Does not listen to warnings of croons
Desert air awaked to sunrise
The man and the woman forever gone.

Clifford Possum Tjapaltjarri

The Healer

Lily Hargraves squints uneasily at the sky:
The rains are heavy this year.
Might be the Rainbow Serpent stirred in her lair.
The weather pattern not really taken into account.
"*El Nino*" effect in the background of city folks
and meteorological data.

Taboos not observed.
Land of ancestors lays untrodden by faithful feet.
People scattered in alien territory.

Rainbow Serpent uncoils from slumber.
Her body gleams in emerging vengeance.
On victims and victors
Unleashed.

The giver of life takes hostages
to its underground world
where the Creative Ancestors wait for the bullroarer's call.

Lily Hargraves Nungarrayi

The twisting body squeezes the helpless shapes.
High-pitched voices rise to the now empty clouds.
On the wet sand still fresh imprints of tiny toes.
Dry sobs escape from behind clenched fists of two kneeling fathers.

Lily Hargraves, in great sorrow, sees only two young girls
floating face down in a muddy billabong left by receding river.
Innocent splashing turned to tears of abandoned mothers.

Lily Hargraves climbs into a truck.
From Lajamanu to Daguragu
Bumpy, treacherous road takes her, and the mourners,
to grieving family gathering.

The future will not shine in two pairs of eyes.
Grevillea flowers will not surround its sweet honey to two eager mouth.
Two future husbands will not meet their promised wives.
Ancestral lines broken in two places.

Lily Hargraves covers her head in ashes.

In another home
Two pale faces gaze through a window.

Young son will not be returning.
Rainbow Serpent flicked its tail.

Future of parents perished in shimmering heat
while mustering cattle on old tribal grounds.
White, ignorant face withering and dissolving in unblinking sun.

Rainbow Serpent's body stretched out
touches two places.
The giver of life takes black and white alike.

Lily Hargraves paints her knowledge on Lajamanu's buildings
Trying to stave the Angel of Death
Her caring brush smears on colours like the blood
painted on doors so long ago in a different desert.

Lily Hargraves Nungarayi lives and paints in Lajamanu

Termite mounds, Tanami Desert

Termite mounds near Daly Waters, Northern Territory

Termite Mounds

Chinese emperor's army frozen in movement on the northern plains.
Turkish women in voluminous galhebiyas going to the market.
Exuberant crowds coming from a football match.
Lunchtime rush of hungry office workers in the city.

Your imagination has a free rein
Whatever you fancy can conjure
Transpose thoughts and bring to life
Mounds of coloured earth.

Rounded towers of crusader's castles,
Minarets of Islam, muezzin's shadow in the folds.
Battle ships, Manhattan skyscrapers.
Anxious mother herding her unruly brood.

From cold and dizzy heights, Machu-Picchu mighty fortress
Teleported to Australia's Tanami Desert swiped by hot winds.
Ready-made compass needle always showing north and south.
Cluster of impatient youngsters waiting to cross the road.

One fertile queen, deep in her chamber
With time on her side to think of involved schemes,
She never sees the efforts of her subjects
And never ventures outside her realm.
Her needs fulfilled to every detail
Absolute ruler, ruled by destiny.

Waving sea of dry spinifex and decaying wood
A ready-made larder and building tool.
Under the chewed up earth a teaming city
Above it, towers, attesting to the power of countless.

Under Ginger Riley's puffed out clouds
Contented Buddhas sprawl ample bodies.
Colonies of featureless spacemen invade Barkly Tablelands.
Shark teeth implanted in irregular rows
On unchanging Cambrian plain.

Dark brown, reddish, in pale ochres, surprisingly white
Sometimes intermingling or claiming exclusive possession.
Big, fat, small, slender, only just beginning or already dead,
Looking left or right, pointing north or south,
Solitary or gregarious, close together or apart.
Inside teaming with life, simulating an abandoned look outside.

A painting by Edward Blitner, 'Jilgirin - Jilgirin' (The Mermaid)

Edward is an artist from the Minyerri Community, near Roper River, in the Northern Territory. He paints in the so-called X-ray style.

Edward Blitner

Flash of a friendly smile,
Strong, brown hands,
Delicate brush,
Criss-cross hatching on linen canvas.
Stories of Roper River leap about
Like silver barramundi in a Top End billabong.

Water lilies spread their round bodies
And display voluptuous white and pink flowers.
Jabiru stalks shallows with an ever-ready eye.
File snake sits at the bottom of the lake.
Majestic brolgas dance an elaborate courtship dance.

Edi Blitner, the Marra-Alawa man
Brushes on the teaming stories with skill and knowledge.
Secrets hidden below the beauty.
Ceremonies passed on.

Edward Blitner

Ada Bird Petyarre with her grand-children

Ada Bird Petyarre with her painting "Mountain Lizard Dreaming"

Ada Bird Petyarre is an artist from Utopia. She is one of seven sisters, all of them painters.

Ada Petyarre

Ada Petyarre's old hand is gliding
So lovingly on coloured lines.
She tries to explain in few simple words
A lifetime of dances and dreams.

She lifts her head from the canvas
And dips a brush in the paint
The spirit of her ancestors
Flows from her capable hands.

"Awelye" the women are dancing
Men's singing comes from the bush
The young girls' bodies are bending
To rhythms of ancient dreams.

Ada Bird Petyarre

Sturt's Desert Pea, Strzelecki Desert, South Australia.

An exhibition viewed at the right time can do wonders for one's well being.

The Two Petyarre Sisters- Gloria and Nancy

Rainy and grey Melbourne day in June.
Soul drips with melancholy.
Thoughts won't leave the confines of your skull,
Not even to try to grope their way towards your open eyes.

Hard streets, dirty puddles, naked foreign trees.
Umbrellas blown in your face.
Rounded shoulders, bleak spirits.
Desperation looking for a way out.

A little notice in a daily paper
Promising an interest and some consolation.
Seems that a Brunswick Street gallery might have answers
For your desultory steps.

Inconspicuous looking door
Scratched and forbidding yields when pushed.
The sunshine, straight from the Centre,
Jumps at you from the walls.

The gloom slowly dissolving.
Cicadas start to sing in your innards.
Exhaled air whizzes past clenched teeth
You feel muscles stretching into a smile.

Gloria and Nancy Petyarre
Still with red dust in their breath
Exude warmth and openness of the desert
Matronly bodies firmly entrenched in the chairs.

They sit in the gallery unperturbed
Drinking tea and eating dates
Colourful woollen jumpers
Keeping the city cold at bay.

Nancy, Margo and Gloria

Emily Kame Kngwareye, behind her Lily Sandover

Emily Kame Kngwarreye was an Aboriginal artist of world stature. Art critics admired her silk batiks and then her canvasses. Connoisseurs of fine art and all who came to know her painting were spell-bound by their beauty. Emily was also a noted stockwoman in her youth.

Emily Kame Kngwarreye

Callouses on fingers
Hard muscles from holding reins.
Wide brimmed hat
Now thrown in the dust
And trampled by unmustered cattle.

A dainty brush.
Gossamer silks.
Smell of wax
Wafting in the crisp desert air.

Emily murmurs
Stories of ancient Dreamings
Dripping colours in myriads of dots.
Swirling flowers emerge in sunlight
To enhance a piece of cloth.

Bent back hurting.
Strong smelling paints.
Irritated nostrils.
Enchanting beauty
Emerges from under hard working hands.

Boldly held brush.
Sweeping strokes.
Impatient mien.
Emily's Alkahere country
Displayed in all seasons and moods.

Butterfly Bush

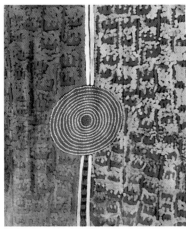

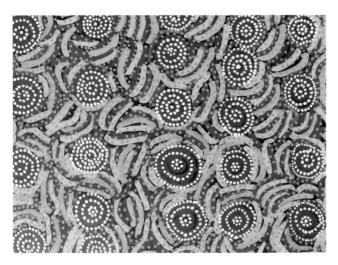

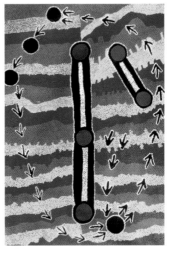

Paintings by: Turkey Tolson
Tjupurrula, Dolly
Nampitjinpa, Ronny
Tjampitjinpa, triptych by
three Tjapaltjarri tribal
brothers: Cassidy, Billy
Stockman and Clifford
Possum, Johnny Warrangula
Tjupurrula, Alan Windroo,
Gabriella Possum Nungarrayi,
Clifford Possum Tjapaltjarri.

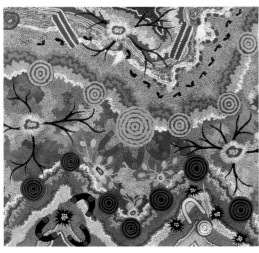
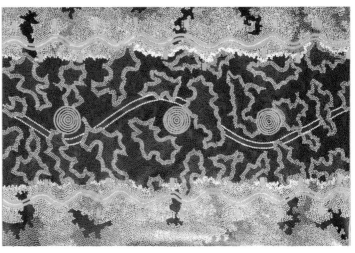

73

On the 30th June 1997, a record price was paid for a painting by an Aboriginal artist, Johnny Warrangula Tjupurrula. It made first page news.

Art Auction

The auction audience gives a thunderous applause.
Not for the artist but for the money
That will pass from one big account to another.

The Dreaming ancestors hover uncertain
If to be glad or not.
Ceremonies and Mimi spirits
Float above the buyer's heads.
The only sound is the clap
Of the auctioneer's hammer.

The prices go up by the thousands.
The desert and river sand still clings to the canvas.
And the yellow drops from the Coolabah cartons
Try to remind the buyers of the artists' pain.

Degraded, unnoticed, pushed away, ridiculed.
Now their art a commodity
To be exchanged, stored, speculated on.

Johnny Warrangula tosses sleeplessly
On the Todd's River cold sand
The long gone Dreaming invading his uneasy thoughts.
Broken, so useless hand, hangs helplessly by his side
Brushes and paints dried out and untouched.

The world is watching the auctioneer's hammer
Brows are sweating, breath withheld.
A price thunders from the rostrum,
Johnny's work *brings home the bacon.*

Far removed from flies and dust storms,
Hungry cries, dirt and slabs of beer.
All is proper, perfumed, polished,
Pecunia non olet, Aboriginal art now sells.

Rock Art in Arnham Land, Northern Territory

How can I ?

How can I feel at home
when my ancestors' bones are buried elsewhere?

In the old country, which I called my own,
the graves are abandoned and overgrown.

Torn between filial duty
and desires to seek the new I climbed a distant shore.

I said goodbye to one then embraced the other,
ancestors' blessings begged in farewell.

But the new land, where I have built my life,
somebody else owned before.

Middens litter the beaches
where I play with my Australian born children.

Scarred trees proclaim past presence
of other people and other lifestyles.

Terra Australis declared *Terra Nullius*, became,
with Edi Mabo, a land with borders and trade routes.

Every part accounted for in stories, dances, songlines.
Ancestral bones bleaching in caves.
In upright coffins sanctified ashes.

So how can I feel at home
without acknowledgment and reconciliation?

*Canoe tree (a tree from which Aborigines, who
lived near the Yarra River, cut away bark for a
canoe), Melbourne, Victoria*

Aboriginal burial caves, Northern Territory

I Had No Shame

I tried to buy your land for a handful of beads.
I was clever.
I tried to own your hunting grounds for few mirrors.
I was enterprising.
I tried to possess the land of your Ancestors.
I was bold.
I tried to wipe out your tribes from this Earth.
I was courageous.
I tried to deny your existence.
I was given credence.
I was clever, enterprising, bold, courageous and trusted.
I had no shame.
Why should I ?
I was bringing civilisation to this barbaric land.
I was told this and I said it.
And when I gloated over my golden riches
I then realised I've become like Midas
And my heart turned cold.

Now I begin slowly to understand that it's you
Who can restore my feelings and my soul.
But can you forgive me ?
Can you forgive someone who had no shame?

Port of Fremantle, Western Australia where the author first glimpsed "Terra Felix"

Paradoxes - 1963

I was a migrant in a land
Where I became a citizen before the original Australian.

I had full rights
Before to them they were given.

The Kooris by indifference hidden
Were to me invisible.

I walked the streets of the big city
Not knowing that the Aborigines were still living.

Derided for not speaking English
I was left powerless and voiceless so not knowing.

I didn't realise then
There were questions to be asked.

That I would discover history
Shaming the 'pillars' of the society.

I would learn words that were not from England
And history that was much older then Europe's.

A rich heritage of people who refused to 'die out'
And so conveniently disappear.

Now I have to ask myself :
Of which country am I citizen?

Was I accepted as a migrant by the first Australians?

The new migrant, Margo in 1963

Princess Pier - the port of disembarkation - Melbourne Victoria. For me and many others a new beginning.

The Family of Ronnie Lawson Jagamarra and Louisa Lawson Napaltjarri, Tanami Desert.

In response to Jack Davies' poem "Integration".

Integration ?

Why integrate Jack
When you lived strong before.
So you say, there is no turning back.
You show us the ajar door
To prove that the world should forget.
Remembering wrongs done and trying to forgive.
Aren't you asking too much of a race neglected
When the pride of people was trampled and ignored ?

Mission bells called for abandonment of old beliefs
Spears of proud nomads broken and discarded
Tjurringa stones defiled and rejected
Spirit broken and confused.
In whose name it all happened?
What right has one race to subjugate another?
We should not ask to integrate but live with each other.

Yes Jack, your poems flow gently like a placid river
But the steep banks threaten the waters below
Turbulent thoughts twist and turn underneath the surface
They'll break free and will demand attention.

Pelicans, The Coorong, South Australia

Written after listening to a concert at "Gasworks" in South Melbourne. One of the singers was Ruby Hunter, an Aboriginal woman from the generation of "Stolen Children".

Coorong Girl

Pelicans flying over my land
Middens sprawling on the shore
Bulrushes bending in the wind
Dark waters of the lake
Painted over by mighty gales.

I feel the Coorong pulling me in
Salty droplets in my hair
The sound in my heart
The shimmer in my eyes.

But I was taken, taken away
From Mother's arms
And Father's strong shadow
Far, far away.

My Coorong, my childhood dream
Fading away in far away land.
Longing for me
My bare feet on warm sand.

Should I be grateful for the veneer?
Pious hands bend in supplications?
Murmuring incessant placebo words,
It's for your own good dear.

I stretch my hand to feel the wind
I lift my eyes to see the sun
I send my thoughts to find again
My happy days, my tribal ways.

Ruby Hunter

Poem inspired by Ruby Hunter and Archie Roach's concert.

Yappa - Sister

Words flowing.
Darkness swallowing shadows.
Young, eager faces intent on understanding
raw sounds of sorrow and pain.

Hands reaching out.
Ears aglow.
Blood pumping strongly
with outrage and shame.

Ruby's words pluck the heart strings.
But hollow, hollow the sound
and wasted appeal
if not answered and taken in.

Sister, sister, yappa, yappa.
Melodic Aboriginal word
caresses young heads
and seeps into open souls.

Archie Roach at the 'Prince of Wales', St Kilda, Victoria

Written after a concert at the "Prince of Wales" in St.Kilda, Victoria.

Archie vs The Audience

Archie:
    Serious eyes.
    Eager words.
Audience:
    Rush of emotions.
    Goose pimples on white skin.
Archie:
    Lips close to the mike.
    Convincing.
Audience:
    Feet tapping.
    Standing up and grabbing sounds.
Archie:
    Sadness revealed.
    Needs not fulfilled.
Audience:
    Enchanted circle of listeners.
    Universal message listened to.
Archie:
    Words of basic desires.
    Freedom, justice, identity.
Audience:
    Thunder of clapping hands.
    Last drink.

Now home.
The gig is over.

Archie Roach

Mimi Spirits, Aboriginal rock paintings, Kakadu, Northern Territory

Ruby Hunter - A Singer

Sparkling signature vest
Hands strumming strings
The guitar nearly her size
Flowing words trying to reach our hearts.

Emus feathers twined in dark hair
Ngarrindjeri-Kukutha's people blood in her veins
Warm tones of crooning voice
Penetrate our subconscious mind.

Such simple way
    a voice
    a guitar
    a heart seeking truth
    showing us the wrongs done
And repetitious words:
"Ain't no time to ever complain"

Ruby, Ruby sing your way
to our hearts.
Let us understand your sadness
and our shame.
Ruby, Ruby sing your songs
and bring us together.
Show us how to right the wrongs.

Ruby Hunter

Spinifex

Women's Corroboree, Mt Liebig. *Photo: G. Wilkins*

Ruby Hunter sings at "The Prince of Wales", St. Kilda, Victoria.

A Pub Gig

Different dreaming
Different sound
Different music
Beating of drums.

No dust is rising
From dancing feet
Fire glows only on cigarette tips.
Sound of glasses
Beat of a drum
No smell of gum leaves
Only of car fumes.

Different rhythm
Different people
Different tune
Dreaming imprisoned in a room.

Ruby Hunter and "The Rotatores"

Tanami Desert, Northern Territory

River gums

Memories on a Table Cloth

In a homely kitchen
in suburban Melbourne
Ruby spreads her arms
on a flowery table-cloth.

She looks at Ngarrindjeri words
written on pieces of paper
hanging next to her stove.

Sounds of silver Murray cod
splashing in flowing water
Shining stars piercing night sky,
hooting of owls invading
stillness of a camp fire.
Crooning of mothers,
whispers of the bush
all crowd on that colourful table-cloth.

Dreamscape

Pakanu-grandfather, *karlo*-day, *ngende*-night, *tinuwarre*-bream, *nyirin*-cry, weep, *kuratye*-Coorong
fish, beautiful Ngarrindjeri words taught to me by Ruby Hunter, a Ngarrindjeri Kukutha woman..

Pakanu

A patient hand of my *Pakanu*
guides unskilled and awkward cast.
Karlo is done, the *ngende* is coming.
A silver *tinuwarre* plops in the lake.
The bush is silent.

Glimmer of fire
jumps from tree to tree.
Kuratye's not biting.
Impatient youth
wriggles on grassy bank.

Pakanu tries to tell a story
of hunting in dear, old days,
but my body is uncomfortable and stiff
I have no patience to listen.

Nyirin, nyirin,
it's now too late
to hear a Dreamtime song,
clapping of sticks, pounding of thighs.
Nyirin, nyirin,
it's too late now
to see the rising dust
from under dancing feet.

My *Pakanu*, my Mother's Father,
has gone to join his Dreamtime ancestors.

Mosaic designed by an Aboriginal artist - Michael Nelson Jagamarra, in front of Australian Parliament, Canberra .

1980's - A Paradox

When the oppressive systems crumbled
The sorrow, that seeped through before
Now flooded four corners of the globe.
With outstretched hands
And holding the flag of "*Solidarity*"
You breached the unjust walls
The paint splattered bricks and mortar
Could not hold the yearnings.
Memories of shattered desires still visible
Torn on barbed wire.
Heavy curtain rent apart
Revealed not only a chink of light
But, dreamed of only before, wide horizon.
Impatient hands, with all the waiting,
Grabbed now every piece of new-found freedom.
Australia, the land of many hopes
Opened its comforting arms
And became one of the eager destinations.
In the "*now*" materialism
Indulged desires could be fulfilled.
In the rush to fulfilment
Ideals were left behind or forgotten
Like umbrellas no longer needed in sunshine.

My compatriots, look around you
Two hundred years of White Australia history to be learned
Thousand of years of Black culture to be acknowledged.

Do not embrace the one Dream
And trample the other Dreaming
With feet running towards the Golden Calf
The dust will settle in your hearts
It will cover your eyes with shiny scales
And you will build new walls around yourselves.

Bottle brush

99